Eternal Love

An inspirational book to help with the journey of grief.

By Cara Barilla

This book is dedicated to my Mother Marie - Josée.

Thank you for showing me that love is eternal.

"Love is forever and your love will remain right there inside and around you."

"Life's more than just a book: You'll see that different stages in life have different chapters, then pages finish and chapters end. You'll soon see that you are coming to the end of the book. Your book will end; Then you'll step back and see that there's the back of the book, a table, a chair, a hallway and a door to never endings."

"When we close our eyes, another dimension will open the door to your loved one."

"The path of grieving has no destination, for life and death are endless."

"Happiness is as endless as sadness.
You have the choice of balance."

"Healing is a lifelong process. Your love will always be there to guide you."

"Adventure awaits; Your love will give you the courage to help you journey your way through your path."

"There are times where you will feel sad, lost and broken. Feel your love and let them be the light to your darkness."

"Love is never lost. Ever. They will always be there and come back to shine through and beside you."

"We are only human; It's ok to not know what happens next. Trust in the process. You will be guided to your best pathway."

"Always use love to help you..."

"It's okay to stand still, it's okay to change rapidly; Move at your own pace through self- trust and you will alight."

"In your book there are sad chapters, unpredictable twists and endings. Don't close the book just yet, keep reading for you still haven't read the conclusion. The author would've wanted you to read 'til the end."

"Loved ones are blessings. They will reflect you. All they will see is the love you still have, and shine it back on you."

"Many people build a spiritual relationship with their passed loved one. Some can feel their presence and be at peace."

"Let your loving surroundings be the light that reminds you that love is eternal."

"Magic is real. Love is real. Both are timeless and unbreakable miracles and can be used like a wand."

"Trust in the light and you will shine."

"You are a blessing. You are a miracle. It's ok if you don't know it, but there's always someone who knows."

"Let your strength fight through your pathway. Guide yourself with self-love and belief. You are more powerful than you think."

"There are times where it's all quiet. There are times where you are alone. We are all meant to experience this. This is one of the many soul challenges of life."

"Your heart will set you free. Close your eyes and thank yourself for your strength."

"Lightness will always shine through darkness. They are the purest gifts to one another. The unconditional passing through will guide you to where you should be."

"You may miss your love; Know that they still see you every day. Close your eyes and feel the same way. Thoughts are real."

"Where is your favourite place? Let your happy place inspire, guide and heal your darkness. Dark places are healthy; for it recognises the happy places and the new beautiful journeys that are awaiting you."

"Life is so short. Blink once goes a milestone, blink twice goes a lifetime. That's the beauty of life."

"Everything in life is temporary. Except life itself."

"Never feel lonely; For the whole universe is within you."

"The nature of life ends. The nature of life begins. When you hold on to love you won't need to measure where you are."

"Embrace now, live in love and let happy memories shine through you."

"In the end we all end up in the same place. Where that is; close your eyes and feel love."

"Love can shine, heal protect and create. Use love in your own language of living and to honour your loved one."

"Life is an illusion & death is an illusion.
For the soul is eternal."

"Your soul can recharge you with life and love. Close your eyes and you will see all that you have loved and that is eternal."

"Nature can heal you & nature can guide you as we are a part of nature."

"Let the purity of life help and heal you; Healing through helping animals and nature can help recharge your energy and give you purpose."

"Unconditional love will last forever. Your love can heal and help others."

"Feeling loss is a natural part of life. It is also an open door to let love back in; The love of family, friends, animals, art, craft and nature can walk into your empty door and nurture your soul."

"Thank yourself each day for getting through this."

"Cherish the beautiful memories you have in your heart; then let those memories inspire you to assist you with your pathway."

"Talk to yourself. You can count on your everlasting spirit to guide you."

"When it's time to come across darkness, there are always moments to appreciate the light."

"When you think of your loved one, what would they of wanted you to do? Embrace the positive guidance through your memories."

"It's ok to still shine, laugh and be at peace;
For this is knowingness of life's eternal
plan."

"Healing through hugs, words, music and craft are more powerful than you could ever imagine."

"It's ok to want to be alone sometimes, even when people are reaching out to you. Let your inner peace and love care for your next steps."

"Gaining a new angelic relationship with your loved one is everlasting, as death has no pain, no hurt and no regrets."

"When I read through my journal of all of the signs you have given me I feel at ease and grateful for still having you communicate with me."

"We had a beautiful relationship here on earth; And now we are having a beautiful relationship while you're in the spiritual dimension."

"Thank you for being my angel who I can call and talk to and know you're listening."

"Time always heals itself for time is forever endless and forever honest."

"Let nature translate messages to you; whenever you feel relaxed near the ocean, calm under rainfall, blissful under the morning sun and even excited through gusts of wind; nature's language can help send you stories, emotion and positive advice for a clearer path."

"Love never dies. It grows stronger the longer you feel away."

"Love and time together can heal every wound."

"Nature sounds are the language of the heavens. Direction of the wind, movement of leaves and feathers, flowing waters, rainbows and whistles are all enchanting miracles and they are here to live with us and within us."

"Re-living the good moments in your mind and heart will always outshine the darkness."

"Your loved one will always love you and will always thank you for the love that you have given them eternally."

"Love always exists in not what is seen, but what is felt within and never forgotten."

"Journaling is the hidden language that prints your soul communication to the heavens."

"Speaking alone out loud is spoken by one, though heard by many and answered by love."

"It is then when you know your prayers have been answered to say thank you out loud. Your love can hear and feel your heartfelt gratitude. For there are many that you can't see who work to help and guide you."

"Angelic communication works in the mysterious ways of communication through feelings of the heart. Purely and simply."

"Journaling your dreams and feelings could heal souls in not just this dimension."

"Believe in love; For love is a miracle and miracles happen each day."

"Speaking alone out loud heals on different planes."

"Give yourself thanks each day; For you are getting through life on a new path. This is a miracle. This is self-love."

"Giving is the universal act of kindness. Sometimes when giving to others you are nourishing your soul with kindness."

"Continue to shine your inner light as bright as you can; your inner passion can add fire inside of you."

"Arts and crafts are soul music; For it changes your rhythm, frequency, mood and tone."

"Recharging inner love; Love can be translated through music, painting, writing, cooking, and craft. What's your creative behaviour of love."

"Don't feel guilty the moment you start to feel better, get on with your routine, laugh or smile. Your love just wants to see love from you."

"There will always be moments when feelings of anger, sadness, guilt, and regret arise. Try to focus on the moments you don't regret. Focus on the laughs, hugs & warmth in your eye contact. This will set you free on a lighter and more loving journey."

"Every time you miss your loved one always remember; if you look in the mirror with unconditional love that's what their love looked like through their view."

"To feel grateful, it's natural to feel negative first. We must always count our blessings for the beautiful moments that were given to us, and to keep them alive through humble and kind, gentle acts of love."

"Numbness is a natural process of loss. When we lose someone we love it's a shock, and doesn't really sink in until late at night or in lonesome times. This is a blessing for a chance to appreciate the love that still physically remains here on this earth. Life is short. love and give with kindness to those who you care about."

"When there is loss, there is an open door to love yourself. Loving yourself through nature, animals, weather and art is priceless and soulful."

"Don't forget to stop and look around every once in a while and thank god for all of your luxuries. Not everyone has a roof over their head."

"Have a day each week to laugh at all the fun and silly times you had."

"Love can't be erased. Love is a permanent universal element."

"When you close your eyes that's where you can truly see love."

"Life is a dream for the afterlife is reality. Both Dimensions intertwine within each other and heal each other. Your current life and life challenge is a blessing as your loved one is still intertwined within you."

"Never underestimate the true healing power of a hug & pure warmth in eye contact."

"Starting new relationships doesn't mean only human relationships. Feel the powerful energy when building new relationships with the trees, the birds, the flowers, the crystals, the fish pond, the wind and the sea."

"Healing can come with healing others, and healing other relationships. Once you realise how short life is, burden in relationships will cease to exist."

"Your love that you have lost is lost by sight and touch, but never lost by heart, mind, soul, frequency and inner journeys."

"There's nothing more healing than shining pure happiness through your eyes."

"Life and death both circulate within the frequency of pure existence. It is the gift of the circle of life that will guide you to your next soul journey."

"How is it possible that in a blink of an eye my loved one is gone forever? They are never gone for they always live inside and around you. Let your heart show you they are still here."

"Don't forget to smile every day; It is your true self, your higher self that loves you unconditionally. When you connect with yourself, you will connect to a higher frequency and heal the soul."

"Pure love will conquer all."

"Each day is precious; Tell your loved ones how you feel for each new second with them is a step to soul healing."

"Life is beautiful; the afterlife is wondrous."

"It's never too late or too early to ask for help and give help."

"Healing oneself is endless."

"Don't forget to show your soul that the purest love of all is within yourself."

"From the day you lose your loved one the emptiness will ever completely be the same and that's okay. This is a journey of living with loss and turning your loved ones life into honour."

"Love is eternal as is spirit."

"Connecting to your loved ones whether they are here or not is the key to self-discovery."

"The beautiful relationship between yourself and your loved one is always remembered and can be brought back again by one single thought."

"Happiness can always be shared. Don't forget to spread what makes you happy."

"When you think of your loved one it's a beautiful feeling. It can be felt in many different dimensions."

"It's not the end of your relationship with your loved one. It is the beginning of your soul relationship, your spiritual relationship; Only communicated through heart. That is one of many superpowers which a human holds within."

"When your loved one leaves you, they leave you with a soulful gift; The unconditional open gift which binds you again to the loved ones that are still here, they grieve with you. Let that open door reconnect and unite you all together once again; for this is the gift from your loved one. The gift that honours them."

"Your loved one has given you the special gift of love. Treasure this gift and be grateful with your honour. Love is everlasting and not many people are given the beautiful gift."

"Be grateful for the new shift in life that your passed on love has given you. This new shift may have brought your family and friends together, changed your way of thinking and may have opened new portals to your life's journey."

"It's okay to feel regret, guilt, sadness, pain and over-thoughts. This is a naturally soul healing process. Your loved one loves you unconditionally. this process will show you how to love unconditionally with no regrets."

"It's never too late to love purely."

"Embrace the beauty of the past, whether positive or negative. The ingredients of the past have taken you to today and will guide your tomorrow."

"Journaling, singing out loud, embracing your creative side and the beauty of daydreaming will help and heal you through your process."

"Whenever you think of your loved one and tear up, remember this is a powerful moment of a spiritual communication."

"There's always time to say "thank you", "I love you" and "I'm grateful."

"As our eyes are known to be the window of the soul, close your eyes and remember their eyes. Souls are eternal and can always reconnect. Anywhere, anytime."

"Whenever there is death, there is life; Not just life and death within souls, but new life opportunities and endings of paths. Embrace this cycle and be grateful for you have been given the gift to opening and closing of life."

"We are all a natural cycle of the everlasting love in existence. Let your love shine through every day for you are connected always to your loved one and love itself."

"Your loved one can naturally guide you through the art of life; Explore your soul through creation. Create, play, adventure and create kindness. This is a loving vibration which is connected to light."

"Your loved ones are there connected to you always. Believe in love and the healing that love brings; For you will remain connected to your loved one eternally."

"When you grieve, the emotion is as unique as a fingerprint. Believe in your own healing pathway with light; for this is the pathway that will live along side."

"It's okay to feel helpless, it's okay to feel out of your natural control. This is your ascension."

"When you trust yourself to live in love and not fear, you are giving yourself back a little piece of your soul."

"There are so many different ways to connect to your inner light. Meditation, affirmation and prayer are tools that can assist in grounding and balancing your soul."

"Let your inner magic guide your path. Use all of your five senses to heal and your heart to breathe in the world."

"The volume of your heart is infinite."

"Blessings to you on this soulful journey."

www.ingramcontent.com/pod-product-compliance
Lightning Source LLC
Chambersburg PA
CBHW060647150426
42811CB00086B/2453/J